Economy Update: 2009

Campbell R. McConnell

University of Nebraska

Stanley L. Brue

Pacific Lutheran University

Sean M. Flynn

Vassar College

 **McGraw-Hill Irwin**

Boston   Burr Ridge, IL   Dubuque, IA   New York   San Francisco   St. Louis
Bangkok   Bogotá   Caracas   Kuala Lumpur   Lisbon   London   Madrid   Mexico City
Milan   Montreal   New Delhi   Santiago   Seoul   Singapore   Sydney   Taipei   Toronto

The McGraw-Hill Companies

McGraw-Hill
Irwin

ECONOMY UPDATE: 2009

Published by McGraw-Hill/Irwin, a business unit of The McGraw-Hill Companies, Inc., 1221
Avenue of the Americas, New York, NY, 10020. Copyright © 2009, 2008, 2005, 2002, 1999, 1996,
1993, 1990, 1987, 1984, 1981, 1978, 1975, 1972, 1969, 1966, 1963, 1960 by
The McGraw-Hill Companies, Inc. All rights reserved. No part of this publication may be reproduced
or distributed in any form or by any means, or stored in a database or retrieval system, without
the prior written consent of The McGraw-Hill Companies, Inc., including, but not limited to, in
any network or other electronic storage or transmission, or broadcast for distance learning.

Some ancillaries, including electronic and print components, may not be available to customers
outside the United States.

This book is printed on acid-free paper.

1 2 3 4 5 6 7 8 9 0 WCK/WCK 0 9

ISBN   978-0-07-734487-0
MHID   0-07-734487-1

www.mhhe.com

The Severe Contraction: An October 2008 through March 2009 Update

To the Student

The purpose of this supplement is to update selected parts of *Economics*, 18e, to account for the U.S. recession that began in December 2007 and worsened toward the end of 2008. The recession resulted from a steep decline in housing prices and a crisis involving mortgage loans and the financial securities built upon them. Several key U.S. financial institutions collapsed or nearly failed, and credit markets largely froze. Despite government bailout efforts, the financial crisis eventually spread to the broader economy.

The economy sputtered through the first three quarters of 2008 before crashing during the last quarter, when real GDP fell by 6.3 percent on an annual basis. By March 2009, employment had declined by 5.8 million workers relative to the start of the recession and the unemployment rate had increased from 4.7 percent in December 2007 to 8.5 percent. The stock market had sunk by roughly

50 percent, and the Federal government had lent hundreds of billions of dollars to bail out failing U.S. financial institutions. Testifying before Congress, Federal Reserve Chair Ben Bernanke referred to the recession as a "severe contraction."

The Severe Contraction—as we will call it—elicited extraordinary public policy measures by the Federal Reserve, the Bush administration, and the new Obama administration. This supplement examines the recession and those policy responses. *But for this material to be helpful, you first need to read and comprehend the analysis in the book's macroeconomics chapters. After reading any particular chapter, please return to this supplement to read the updates that specifically relate to that chapter.* In presenting the updates, we will be referring to specific chapter numbers, page numbers, figure numbers, and table numbers in the book. The updates will provide timely applications and strengthen your understanding of the subject matter. They will be well worth reading!

Keep in mind that this update is only through March 2009. By the time you read *Economics,* subsequent major economic events will surely occur. But the material here will establish a solid base for further updates that may come to you via in-class discussions, data from the Internet, or current publications.

Stanley L. Brue
Sean M. Flynn
Campbell R. McConnell

Chapter 23 (Macro Chapter 6): Introduction to Macroeconomics

1. Banks and Other Financial Institutions (page 470; Macro page 117)

We state in the book that a well-functioning banking system helps to promote economic growth and stability by encouraging saving and channeling it into the most productive possible investments. In the 2007–2009 period, the financial system was certainly *not* well-functioning. Quite the contrary! Lending from banks to households, banks to businesses, and banks to banks largely broke down. The Federal Reserve and U.S. Treasury intervened with huge infusions of money to keep the system from completely freezing up.

2. Uncertainty, Expectations, and Shocks (page 470; Macro page 117)

Figure 23.1 (page 471; Macro Figure 6.1, page 118) illustrates the effect of unexpected changes in demand on the sales of a fictional auto producer (Buzzer) and is designed to illustrate a few key points about the overall economy. This diagram is helpful in introducing the story of the Severe Contraction. Consider Figure 23.1b (Macro Figure 6.1b) where the price of Buzzer's autos is fixed. Like actual auto producers such as GM, Ford, and Chrysler, Buzzer established its production capacity and its expectations of product demand on the basis of normal times. But suppose that demand in this example unexpectedly fell from D_H to D_L because of a general decline in household income, greater difficulty in getting auto loans, and declining consumer confidence. With the price stuck at P, sales of cars would fall from 1,150 to 700 per week. Because fewer workers would be needed to produce fewer cars, Buzzer would need to lay off a large portion of its workforce.

The analysis roughly fits the facts of the Severe Contraction. Between the start of the recession and February 2009, the economy's price level (essentially a weighted average of prices) was quite sticky. In fact, the price level in February 2009 looked very much like the price level in December 2007. Therefore, real output took the full brunt of the decline of total demand in the economy.

Chapter 24 (Macro Chapter 7): Measuring Domestic Output and National Income

1. Putting It All Together: GDP $= C + I_g + G + X_n$ (page 485; Macro page 132)

In the fourth quarter of 2008, real GDP contracted by 6.3 percent on an annual basis. (The adjustment from a quarterly basis to an annual basis simply shows what the three-month decline would equate to if it were to continue for an entire year.) We can use national income and product account data to break down this percentage change. Examine Table 24.3 (page 485; Macro Table 7.3, page 132), where the Receipts: Expenditures Approach in the left column becomes our guide. Now examine the table on page 5 of this supplement. Unlike the numbers in Table 24.3 (Macro Table 7.3), the percentages here are for inflation-adjusted expenditures since inflation adjustments are needed to show declines in *real* expenditures and output.

Percentage Change for Real GDP from Quarter 3, 2008, to Quarter 4, 2008 (Annual Basis) Receipts: Expenditures Approach

GDP Expenditure Components	Percentage Change (Annual basis)
Personal consumption expenditures (C)	−4.3%
Gross domestic investment (I_g)	−23.0
Government purchases (G)	+1.3
Net exports (X_n)	−6.1
Real GDP	−6.3

The 6.3 percent decline in real GDP on an annualized basis reflected a very steep decline of 23 percent in gross investment expenditures, along with less severe but nevertheless contractionary declines in net exports and personal consumption expenditures. The government purchases category was the only spending category to rise during this period and this increase was not large enough to offset the declines in the other components of GDP.

2. The Circular Flow Revisited (page 488; Macro page 135)

Viewed through the circular flow diagram on page 489 (Figure 24.3; Macro Figure 7.3, page 136), the recent recession can be thought of as a pronounced slowing of the main spending and income flows. In particular, U.S. businesses reduced investment expenditures and households reduced personal consumption expenditures. GDP, NDP, NI, and PI therefore all declined. A $100 billion tax rebate program bolstered the consumption flow and increased real GDP in mid 2008, but this larger flow was short-lived. In the fourth quarter of 2008, the main flows in the diagram decreased significantly.

Chapter 25 (Macro Chapter 8): Economic Growth

1. Production Possibilities Analysis (page 506; Macro page 153)

Economic growth became negative (real GDP declined) during the Severe Contraction. That contrasted with the long-term 3.4 percent annual increase of real GDP since 1950. The recession reduced real output, not the economy's production capacity. The production of goods and services simply dropped well below the level of production that the economy was capable of producing.

Figure 25.2 (Macro Figure 8.2) helps clarify this distinction. The nation's production possibilities curve shifted rightward during the recession, reflecting ongoing improvements in labor productivity and an increasing labor force. But due to the recession, the economy did not reach its new, higher potential. It moved from producing at a point like *a* on production possibilities curve *AB* to a point like *c*, which is to the left of production possibilities curve *CD*. Then, the economy declined from point *c* to some point (not shown) even further inside curve *CD*. This latter decline in the production of both consumer goods and capital goods illustrates the recession.

If economic downturns are long enough and deep enough, however, they can negatively affect the subsequent growth of production possibilities. Long periods of idle capital and labor can have carryover effects on the growth rate in subsequent years through the adverse effects they have on the supply factors of growth. For example, recessions depress investment and capital accumulation. Furthermore, the expansion of research budgets may be slowed by recession so that technological advance diminishes; union resistance to technological advance may stiffen; public support for free international trade may weaken; and the skills of idle workers may erode. Although it is difficult to quantify the impact of these considerations on the long-term growth trend, they could take on considerable importance if the current recession carries on for a long time.

2. The Recent Productivity Acceleration (page 511; Macro page 158)

The rate of productivity growth in 2008 (2.7 percent) matched the 2.7 percent annual trend-line growth of productivity since 1995. So, the recession had not altered the recent long-run productivity trend shown as the right blue line in Figure 25.5 (page 511; Macro Figure 8.5, page 158). But this rise in labor productivity in 2008 must be interpreted cautiously. It may have resulted from increased efficiency through better technology, or perhaps simply from firms letting go their least productive workers so that average productivity went up. But to the extent that productivity is the driver of long-run growth, the continued rise in measured productivity in 2008 is encouraging for the future.

Chapter 26 (Macro Chapter 9): Business Cycles, Unemployment, and Inflation

1. Phases of the Business Cycle (page 521; Macro page 168)

Viewed through Figure 26.1 (page 521; Macro Figure 9.1, page 168), the previous economic expansion (first upward blue arrow) that began in 2002 ended in December 2007. The economy then entered a recession phase of the business cycle, as stylized by the second downward red arrow. In March 2009, economists were projecting that the recession phase of the cycle might last for two or more quarters, meaning that the recession had not yet reached its trough. Once reached, this cyclical low point would be followed by renewed expansion, as shown by the second upward blue arrow in the diagram.

The recession has temporarily slowed and halted the rate of U.S. economic growth, but economists expect the rate of growth to move back toward the longer-term growth trend as the economy recovers. Steep recessions are usually followed by steep expansions. But there are no guarantees in business-cycle forecasting!

The latest recession is the sharpest and longest recession since 1982, leading observers to wonder if the economy is experiencing a *depression*. No official dividing line exists between a severe recession and a depression, but the majority of economists would agree that a depression has occurred when a recession has lasted three or more years, real GDP has declined by 10 percent or more, and the unemployment rate has reached 10 percent or higher. Through March 2009, the current recession had lasted 15 months. Real output had declined less than 3 percent, and unemployment had reached 8.5 percent (in February 2009).

Economists do not expect the current recession to become a depression on the magnitude of the Great Depression of the 1930s. Then, real GDP fell by 27 percent in three years and the unemployment rate rose to nearly 25 percent of the labor force.

A final point merits mention. When economists express that a recession has ended, the general public and media sometimes accuse them of "having their heads in the sand" because the economy is still in such bad shape. But, for economists, a recession ends when real GDP begins a sustained increase. The economy may still be "bad" in the sense that unemployment is still high and the economy has a long way to expand before reaching full employment, but "bad economy" and "recession" are not synonymous terms to economists.

2. Figure 26.1: U.S. Recessions since 1950 (page 521; Macro page 168)

The official declaration of the start of the recession occurred after the publication of our book. References throughout the macro chapters therefore are to the economic "slowdown" of 2007 and 2008. The National Bureau of Economic Research (NBER)—a nonprofit economic research organization—has a Business Cycle Dating Committee of prominent macroeconomists that monitors the economy and declares the start and end of recessions. Citing evidence of declining real output and falling employment, the NBER officially declared the start date of the current recession as December 2007.

In Figure 26.1, page 521 (Macro Figure 9.1, page 168), simply add "2007" at the bottom of the first column, with question marks at the bottom of columns 2 and 3. Through March 2009, the recession had lasted 15 months and real GDP had declined by less than 3 percent. (Search **www.nber.org** to see if the NBER's Business Cycle Dating Committee has declared an end to the recession.)

3. Causation: A First Glance (page 522; Macro page 169)

We mention several possible general causes of recession in the book but discuss none in detail because the material is introductory. But of the explanations listed, the best fit for the latest recession is the one that suggests that business cycles can result from unexpected financial bubbles and bursts, which spill over through optimism and pessimism to affect the production of goods and services. The latest recession was precipitated by a severe financial crisis involving overvalued real estate and unsustainable mortgage debt. This debt was bundled into new securities ("derivatives"), which were then sold to financial investors. The investors in turn bought insurance against losses that might arise from the securities. As real estate prices plummeted and mortgage defaults rocketed to levels much higher than had been generally expected, the securitization and insurance structure buckled and nearly collapsed.

4. Cyclical Impacts: Durables and Nondurables (page 522; Macro page 169)

True to our discussion in the book, the latest recession has taken its greatest toll on capital goods (for example, housing, commercial buildings, and heavy equipment) and consumer durables (for example, automobiles, personal computers, and refrigerators). While the output of nondurable consumer goods and services also has declined, the reduction has not been as great as for capital goods and consumer durables. For example, in the fourth quarter of 2008, the outputs of capital goods and consumer durables declined on an annual basis by 22.0 percent and 22.1 percent, respectively. Contrast that to the decline in output of consumer nondurables of 9.4 percent and the increase in services of 1.5 percent. (These data are subject to future revision by the Bureau of Economic Analysis, **www.bea.gov**).

5. Unemployment (page 523; Macro page 170)

Both the number of people unemployed and the unemployment rate increase during recessions. In fact, these rises are one of the important factors that the NBER committee assesses in declaring the start of a recession. The added unemployment during recession is mainly cyclical unemployment (page 525; Macro page 172), not frictional or structural. People lose their jobs because their employers face declining sales. Decreased sales and revenue mean rising inventories, production cuts, reduced employment, and cyclical unemployment.

6. Figure 26.2: The Labor Force, Employment, and Unemployment (page 523; Macro page 170)

Figure 26.2 (Macro Figure 9.2, page 170) provides a good conceptual framework for examining the employment declines and unemployment increases that occurred between the start of the recession in December 2007 and the latest data available for this update (March 2009).

Ignore people who are "under 16 and/or institutionalized" or are "not in labor force." Focus instead on the Labor force section of the diagram which comprises the Employed and Unemployed elements. The table below compares the categories for the two months.

A Comparison of Labor Force Statistics before and during the Recession

(November 2007; millions)	(March 2009; millions)
Total labor force = 153.9	Total labor force = 154.0
Employed = 146.7	Employed = 140.9
Unemployed = 7.2	Unemployed = 113.2
Unemployment rate = 4.7%	Unemployment rate = 8.5%

Between these two periods, unemployment increased by more than 5 million people and the unemployment rate jumped from 4.7 percent to 8.5 percent. At this time (March 2009), the recession's trough is not in sight. The general consensus is that the employment and unemployment numbers will worsen before they improve.

Be advised that unemployment rates sometimes rise for a while even after an economic expansion resumes. During the recession, many people who cannot find jobs become discouraged and drop out of the labor force. Therefore, they are *not* officially unemployed and not included in the unemployment rate. In the early phase of the expansion, these workers reenter the labor force to look for new jobs. During their job search, they *are* officially unemployed. So the unemployment rate may temporarily rise even as the economy picks up. At some point, the increase in hiring overpowers the reentry of previously discouraged workers and the unemployment rate drops.

7. Figure 26.3: Actual and Potential GDP (page 527; Macro Figure 9.3, page 174)

In Figure 26.3a (Macro Figure 9.3a), extending the plotting of the data through March 2009 would drop the blue line showing actual real GDP well below the red line showing potential GDP. The latest recession has caused a negative GDP gap. In Figure 26.3b (Macro Figure 9.3b) we would show the substantial cyclical unemployment accompanying this negative GDP gap as a distinct upward spike in the blue line. The recession is particular costly to people who lose their jobs but also very costly to society. Society loses billions of dollars of output (and income).

8. Unequal Burdens (page 526; Macro page 173)

Unemployment rates for some categories of workers increase more rapidly during recession than for other categories. This is the point of Table 26.2 (Macro Table 9.2), in which less-than-full-employment year 2002 (column 1) and full-employment year 2007 (column 2) are compared.

A comparison of unemployment rates between full-employment year 2007 and recession-year 2008 would show similar tendencies. In particular, the recent recession has disproportionately increased unemployment rates for construction workers, manufacturing workers, and retail workers. In contrast to previous recessions, it has boosted the unemployment rates of whites by a larger percentage than for African-Americans. Also, it has increased the male unemployment rate by more than the female unemployment rate.

9. Facts of Inflation (page 530; Macro page 177)

The recession has reduced the total demand for goods and services and therefore removed the demand-pull inflation that was beginning to occur in 2007. On a December-to-December basis, the Consumer Price Index in the United States rose by only 0.1 percent in 2008. Plotting the inflation rate for 2008 in Figure 26.4 (Macro Figure 9.4) therefore would produce a sharp downward spike of the line from the 4.1 percent in 2007 to a position just above the horizontal axis. Inflation also has declined in the other industrial nations highlighted in the Global Perspective on page 530 (Macro page 177).

The decline in the rate of inflation to near zero has generated a concern that deflation may occur for the first time since 1955. The Federal Reserve (the U.S. central bank) wants to prevent deflation and has taken aggressive steps to try to make sure that it does not occur. These steps involve aspects of monetary policy, which is the subject of Chapter 33 (Macro Chapter 16) and our updates for that chapter.

Why the concern about deflation? First, it typically occurs only when the economy is falling deeper into a recession. It therefore reflects an underlying malady of deficient aggregate spending and confirms that public policy has failed to halt the decline in the economy. Deflation also can worsen a recession by further undermining the already diminished willingness of households and businesses to borrow and spend. When the price level is falling, dollars borrowed do not have as much purchasing power as the dollars needed to pay back the loans. Borrowing is thus discouraged, even though nominal interest rates may sink to zero. Also, expectations of falling prices cause households and businesses to wait for prices to fall farther before purchasing consumer and capital goods. This behavior reduces current demand and thus makes the recession worse.

10. Last Word: The Stock Market and the Economy (page 536; Macro page 183)

As pointed out in this Last Word, stock market crashes can hurt the economy. This point has been borne out by recent events. The Dow Jones Industrial Average declined 19 percent during the last three months of 2008 and was down nearly 34 percent for the entire year. Stock prices continued to plummet in early 2009, falling another 25 percent through March 9. This decline engendered overall economic pessimism and also produced a huge negative wealth effect that undoubtedly reduced consumer spending. Finally, lower stock prices meant that any stock sold by companies attempting to raise funds to purchase new capital would only bring in a much smaller amount of money. Lower stock prices therefore constrained the ability of firms to expand their operations by selling stock.

Chapter 27 (Macro Chapter 10): Basic Macroeconomic Relationships

1. The Income-Consumption and Income-Saving Relationships (page 542; Macro page 189)

The Severe Contraction has at least temporarily altered the consumption and saving behavior in the economy. Concerned about high debt and potential job losses, households have increased their saving and reduced their consumption spending at each level of disposable (after-tax) income. In Figure 27.2 (page 544; Macro Figure 10.2, page 191), we would show this change of behavior as a downward shift of the consumption schedule in the top graph and an upward shift of the saving schedule in the lower graph.

This change of behavior illustrates the *paradox of thrift*. The irony is that saving more is *good* for the economy in the long run because it finances investment and therefore fuels subsequent economic growth. But saving can be *bad* for the economy during a recession, when the increased saving is unlikely to be matched by an equal amount of investment. The extra saving then simply reduces spending on goods and services. That means that even more businesses suffer, more layoffs occur, and income declines even more.

Even worse, households as a group may inadvertently end up saving less by trying to save more during a recession. Their reduced spending creates more job losses and further drives down total income. The decline in total income makes it very difficult for an economy to save as much as it did before the spending and income reductions.

2. The Interest-Rate–Investment Relationship (page 548; Macro page 195)

During the recent recession, real interest rates declined to near zero or even perhaps below zero. Figure 27.5 (page 550; Macro Figure 10.5, page 197) suggests that this drop in interest rates should have boosted investment spending. But just the opposite happened. As we previously stated, investment spending declined 23 percent in the fourth quarter of 2008 alone. What gives? Toss out the figure?

Definitely not! The key to the riddle is that during the recession the investment demand curve shifted inward, as from ID_0 to ID_2 in Figure 27.6 (page 551; Macro Figure 10.6, page 198), to such an extent that this shift overmatched any investment-increasing effects of the decline in real interest rates. The result was less investment, not more.

The leftward shift of the investment demand reflects a decline in the expected returns from investment. As indicated in "Stock of Capital Goods on Hand" (page 552; Macro page 199), firms see little or zero returns on investment in new capital when they have an overstock of existing capital relative to their current sales. They therefore are not inclined to invest.

The section "Expectations" (page 552; Macro page 199) is also relevant. During the recession, firms became very pessimistic about when the economy would regain its strength. That also contributed to low expected rates of return on investment and extremely weak investment demand.

3. Figure 27.7: The Volatility of Investment (page 553; Macro Figure 10.7, page 200)

The recent recession reinforces the central point of Figure 27.7 (Macro Figure 10.7): Economic investment (in real terms) is extremely volatile relative to real GDP. For example, while real GDP declined by 6.3 percent on an annual basis in the fourth quarter of 2008, investment spending declined by 23 percent on an annual basis.

4. The Multiplier Effect (page 554; Macro page 201)

Table 27.3 (page 555; Macro Table 10.3, page 202) provides helpful insights on how output and income increases during an economic expansion can enlarge like a snowball rolling down a snowy slope.

During a recession like the present one, however, the analysis runs in the opposite direction. To see how this works, simply place a minus sign in front of all the numbers in the table. The decline in investment spending of $5 billion means that households collectively have $5 billion less income. With an MPC of .75 and an MPS of .25, that $5 billion reduction of income in the first round of the multiplier process reduces consumption by $3.5 billion (= $5 billion × .75). Saving declines by $1.25 billion (= $5 billion × .25).

The $3.5 billion decline in consumption in turn reduces income in the second round of the multiplier process by $3.5 billion, which further reduces consumption by $2.82 billion (= $3.75 × .75). Observe that income and consumption go down in successive rounds until eventually income has declined by $20 billion. In this table (with minus signs), the $5 billion investment decline has driven down income by $20 billion, or by four times the initial decline in investment. The multiplier in this textbook example therefore is 4 (= $20/5). Here it is negative.

The real-world relevancy is that once an initial decline in spending occurs, it can feed upon itself, making matters worse in the economy. That seems to have occurred in the latest recession. But be aware that the size of the multiplier in the U.S. economy is not known. Some economists think it may be 1.5 or even lower; others suggest that it could be as high as 3 or more. The multiplier is also highly germane to attempts to use tax cuts and government spending increases to create spending increases that ripple through the economy. We will say more on this subject after you have read Chapter 30 (Macro Chapter 13) on fiscal policy.

5. Last Word: Squaring the Economic Circle (page 557; Macro page 204)

Be sure to read this Last Word. Written over 30 years ago, it is remarkably relevant to the role the multiplier has played in the Severe Contraction.

Chapter 28 (Macro Chapter 11): The Aggregate Expenditures Model

1. Recessionary Expenditure Gap (Page 575; Macro page 222)

The current recession is easily portrayed through the aggregate expenditures model, which John Maynard Keynes (1883–1946) created to explain the Great Depression of the 1930s. Examine Figure 28.7a on page 576 (Macro Figure 11.7a, page 223). Recall that the AE_0 line in this figure consists of the combined amount of after-tax consumption expenditures (C_a), gross investment expenditures (I_g), net export expenditures (X_n), and government purchases (G) planned at each level of real GDP. During the Severe Contraction, both after-tax consumption and investment expenditures declined, with the largest drop being investment expenditures.

As viewed through the figure, aggregate expenditures thus declined, as from AE_0 to AE_1. This set off a multiple decline in real GDP, illustrated in the figure by the decline from $510 billion to $490 billion. In the language of the aggregate expenditures model, a recessionary expenditure gap produced a sizeable negative GDP gap. Employment sank, unemployment rose, and the unemployment rate bolted upward.

2. Keynes' Solution to a Recessionary Expenditure Gap (page 575; Macro page 222)

Keynes' solution to a recessionary expenditure gap sheds significant light on the actual U.S. policies undertaken in 2008 and 2009 to try to eliminate the recessionary expenditure gap facing the economy at that time. In 2008, the government provided $100 billion of tax rebate checks to taxpayers, hoping those getting them would spend a large portion of their checks. In 2009 a $787 billion stimulus package was enacted to boost aggregate expenditures to try to reduce the recessionary expenditure gap and, through the multiplier effect, increase real GDP and employment. We will defer discussion of these stimulus attempts until our updates for Chapter 30 (Macro Chapter 13) on fiscal policy, but it is easy to see their purpose from Figure 28.7a (Macro Figure 11.7a). If aggregate expenditures can be driven up from AE_1 toward AE_0, the recession will end and the recovery phase of the business cycle will begin.

3. International Economic Linkages (page 570; Macro page 217)

We are backtracking in page order but the discussion of international linkages applies to the U.S. recession. The severe downturn in the United States reduced U.S. imports (other nation's exports). Countries such as Canada and Japan—whose economies depend highly on exports to the United States—therefore were negatively impacted by the U.S. recession. These countries, along with many others, suffered from their own financial crises and domestic weaknesses, and the decline in sales to the United States helped push them into recession. As their respective recessions made them poorer, they cut back on their purchases of U.S. exports. That, in turn, further lowered real GDP in the United States.

Global recessions typically shrink the volume of international trade. This reduces the output gains from specialization and exchange and, therefore, lowers global output and income. That is precisely what has happened during the current recession. The World Trade Organization has projected that world trade will shrink by 9 percent in 2009, the largest collapse since the Second World War.

As pointed out in the Tariffs section of the book (page 570; Macro page 217), nations experiencing painful declines in employment often are tempted to impose tariffs on imports to protect domestic production and employment. But when one trading partner increases trade barriers, other partners normally retaliate. To keep recessions from worsening, trading partners need to resist trade restrictions as well as other protectionist behaviors, such as enacting laws requiring that their governments buy goods only from domestic producers. These policies may for a time be good politics, but they are bad economics. They result in even greater unemployment and hardship.

Chapter 29 (Macro Chapter 12): Aggregate Demand and Aggregate Supply

1. Chapter Introduction (page 583; Macro page 230)

The chapter introduction in the book ends with a reference to the attempt to use public policy in 2008 "to try to prevent recession." In fact, we now know that a recession actually began in December 2007 and worsened in the last quarter of 2008.

2. Decreases in AD: Recession and Cyclical Unemployment (page 596; Macro page 243)

The text's discussion relating to Figure 29.9 (page 596; Macro Figure 12.9, page 243) helps demonstrate the Severe Contraction. A large unexpected decrease in aggregate demand (as from AD_1 to AD_2) occurred because private-sector spending suddenly declined. Viewed through the determinants of aggregate demand (the table on page 586; Macro page 233):

- *Consumer spending* declined because of (a) reduced consumer wealth due to large reductions in real estate values and stock market values, (b) diminished consumer expectations about future employment and income levels, and (c) increased emphasis on saving more and borrowing less.
- *Investment spending* declined because of lower expected returns on investment. These lower expectations resulted from the prospects of poor future business conditions and high degrees of excess capacity.

The decline in aggregate demand jolted the U.S. economy from a point such as *a* in Figure 29.9 (Macro Figure 12.9) leftward to a point such as *b*. Because the price level remained roughly constant, the decline in aggregate demand caused the economy to move leftward along the immediate-short-run aggregate supply curve (the dashed horizontal line). As a result, real GDP took the brunt of the blow, declining sharply (as from Q_f to Q_1). By contrast, if prices had been more flexible, then the economy could have slid down the downward-sloping AS curve (as from point *a* to point *c*), with the result being a smaller decrease in real GDP (as from Q_f to Q_2). But with the price level roughly constant, a full-strength multiplier occurred, as illustrated in Figure 29.9 by the decline of output from Q_f to Q_1, rather than from Q_f to Q_2. As of March 2009, the U.S. economy was experiencing a huge negative GDP gap (as illustrated by Q_1 minus Q_f in the figure), which was accompanied by a large reduction in employment, a large increase in unemployment, and a sharp rise in the unemployment rate.

3. Last Word: Has the Impact of Oil Prices Diminished? (page 599; Macro page 246)

At the very end of this Last Word, we point out that the price of oil rose from slightly over $50 a barrel in January 2007 to more than $140 a barrel in July 2008. The concern was that the dramatic rise of oil prices might increase the per-unit production costs of output and reduce aggregate supply. This could spark cost-push inflation or, worse, stagflation.

Neither of these occurred. The rise of oil prices instead turned out to be a speculative bubble that burst when world economies slowed. The price of oil fell by about as much and as fast as it had just shot upward. In March 2009, the price was $40 a barrel.

This episode is a good reminder of the need to distinguish carefully between rapidly rising (or falling) prices of commodities such as oil, copper, gold, wheat, corn, or cattle over short periods of time and the long-term trend of these erratic commodity prices. The rise and fall of oil prices over those two years also confirms the main point of this Last Word: Changes in oil prices—even spectacular ones—seem to have less of an effect on aggregate supply than they once did.

Chapter 30 (Macro Chapter 13): Fiscal Policy, Deficits, and Debt

1. Expansionary Fiscal Policy (page 608; Macro page 255)

The recession prompted the Federal government to use fiscal policy to try to increase aggregate demand, output, and employment. Both policy measures are easily understood via Figure 30.1 (page 608; Macro Figure 13.1, page 255).

We have already stated the features of the Economic Stimulus Act of 2008 in the book, but we now can say more. Recall that this legislation established tax rebates (stimulus payments) for people who filed a 2007 tax return and met specific eligibility requirements. The maximum stimulus payment was $600 for single persons and $1,200 for married couples, plus $300 for each child. But stimulus payments also decreased with incomes, so that higher-income individuals and couples did not receive stimulus checks at all.

About $100 billion of the $152 billion package consisted of stimulus checks that were designed to increase aggregate demand, real output, and employment. As viewed through the AD-AS model of Figure 30.1 (Macro Figure 13.1), the idea was to shift the aggregate demand curve from some position such as curve AD_2 to the broken line immediately to its right. This shift represents the initial added consumption spending resulting from the stimulus checks. Through the multiplier effect, the eventual increase in aggregate demand would end up at AD_1, causing real GDP and output to expand as shown. With the expansion, employment would rise and the unemployment rate would fall.

The policy worked to expand output in the second quarter of 2008 and perhaps dampened the modest decline of output in the third quarter of 2008. But the stimulus plan was not as expansionary or long-lasting as anticipated. Because the financial situation in many households was so precarious, many people who received

the checks used them to pay down existing debt or saved the funds because of uncertainty about maintaining their jobs. Therefore, the initial rightward shift of the AD curve was somewhat muted. Also, because this same behavior also occurred in the subsequent rounds of the multiplier process, the overall impact on real output was diminished. After the fiscal stimulus had temporarily propped up the receding economy, real GDP continued to fall. The forces of recession completely overwhelmed the fiscal policy.

The second round of antirecessionary fiscal policy is set to arrive in 2009 and 2010. With the economy continuing its precipitous slide, the Obama administration and Congress enacted the American Recovery and Reinvestment Act in early 2009. This gigantic $787 billion program consisted of low- and middle-income tax rebates, plus large increases in expenditures on infrastructure, education, and health care. The idea was to flood the economy with additional spending to try to boost aggregate demand and get people back to work.

The tax cuts in the package were aimed at lower- and middle-income individuals and households, who were thought to be more likely than high-income people to spend (rather than save) the extra income from the tax rebates. Lower- and middle-income households generally have higher marginal propensities to consume than richer people. Rather than sending out lump-sum stimulus checks as in 2008, the new tax rebates were to show up as small increases in workers' monthly payroll checks. With smaller amounts per month rather than a single large check, it was hoped that people might spend the bulk of their enhanced income—rather than save much of it as they had done with the one-time-only, lump-sum checks received in 2008.

The second part of the fiscal policy (60 percent of the funding) consisted of increases in government expenditures. As we indicate in the book (Current Thinking on Fiscal Policy, page 618; Macro page 265), most economists believe that fiscal policy should be held in reserve for recessions that appear to be deep and long-lasting. The Severe Contraction certainly qualifies in that regard.

The Congressional Budget Office (CBO) estimates that the fiscal package will boost real GDP by 1 to 3 percentage points above what it would have been otherwise. They estimate that the stimulus package will reduce the unemployment rate by .5 to 2 percentage points. Skeptics say that the package will mainly increase the size and scope of government, impede the private sector, and lower the nation's long-run rate of economic growth.

2. Automatic or Built-In Stabilizers (page 612; Macro page 259)

The automatic stabilizers discussed in this section have kicked in during the recession but have not had sufficient force to offset the overall plunge in aggregate demand. The decline in personal income has automatically reduced income tax revenues. Declines in the values of houses and stock shares have produced capital losses, so tax revenues from the capital gains tax are way down. The decline in corporate profits has automatically reduced the tax inflow to government from the corporate income tax. Falling consumer spending has lowered sales tax revenues received by state and local governments.

As viewed through Figure 30.3 (page 612; Macro Figure 13.3, page 259), the decline in taxes resulting from the reduction of GDP has automatically increased the size of the Federal budget deficit.

Consequently, part of the rapidly rising Federal budget deficit is cyclical and unrelated to the two major fiscal stimulus packages.

3. Table 30.1: Federal Deficits (−) and Surpluses (+) as Percentages of GDP, 1992–2007 (page 614; Macro Table 13.1, page 261)

As a percentage of GDP, the Federal budget deficit was −3.2 percent in 2008, up sharply from the −1.3 percent listed for 2007 in Table 30.1 (Macro Table 13.1). This increase resulted from the automatic drop-off of tax revenues just discussed, along with the tax rebates (fiscal stimulus checks) paid out in 2008. As a percentage of potential GDP, the standardized budget deficit rose from −1.4 percent in 2007 to −2.5 percent in 2008. This increase reveals that fiscal policy in 2008 was expansionary. It will be even more expansionary in 2009 and perhaps also in 2010.

4. Budget Deficits and Projections (page 615; Macro page 262)

The recession and the stimulus packages have already rendered the projected deficits and surpluses shown in Figure 30.5 (page 616; Macro Figure 13.5, page 263) obsolete. For example, the actual deficit for 2008 was $455 billion, much higher than the $219 billion projected in the figure.

Here are the new projections for updating the figure, all in millions of nominal dollars: 2009 = −1,390; 2010 = −703; 2011 = −498; 2012 = −264; 2013 = −257; 2014 = −250. Some observers think that the deficit for 2009 may reach even higher, perhaps to $1.8 trillion. You can check for updates at **www.cbo.gov** (Budget Projections).

5. Offsetting State and Local Finance (page 618; Macro page 265)

In the text we point out why the fiscal policies of state and local government often are pro-cyclical and thus intensify rather than moderate recessions. The $787 billion fiscal package of 2009 made a special effort to reduce this problem by giving aid dollars to state governments. Because of the Federal aid, the states will not have to increase taxes and reduce expenditure as much as otherwise. So their collective fiscal actions will not fight against the increase in aggregate demand that the Federal government wants to achieve with its tax cuts and expenditure increases.

6. The Public Debt (page 619; Macro page 266)

The $455 billion Federal budget deficit in 2008 and the projected deficit for 2009 of $1,390 billion will increase the size of the public debt, both absolutely and relatively. The public debt is projected to rise to $11.5 trillion in 2009, up from $9.01 trillion in 2007. As a percentage of GDP, the portion of the public debt that is held by the public (not held by state governments, Federal agencies, or the Federal Reserve) also will rise. If plotted in Figure 30.7 (page 620; Macro Figure 13.7, page 267), this would produce a sizeable uptick in the red line for 2008 and 2009.

7. Figure 30.8: The Investment Demand Curve and the Crowding-Out Effect (page 622; Macro Figure 13.8, page 269)

Critics of the $787 billion fiscal stimulus package are fearful that the borrowing needed to finance it and the resulting large rise in the public debt will bode ill for private investment spending, which is the main engine of long-term economic growth. Because of the deficit and debt, interest rates may eventually rise and crowd out private investment spending. This potential outcome is illustrated in Figure 30.8 (Macro Figure 13.8) by first examining investment demand curve ID_1, where the rise in the real interest rate from 6 percent to 10 percent reduces investment from $25 billion to $15 billion. With less private investment in new capital, the economy's production possibilities will not expand in future years by as much as they would if there were no crowding out.

Proponents of the stimulus package counter that investment has declined even though the real interest rate has fallen to zero. They say that current recessionary circumstances largely preclude the stimulus package from crowding out private investment. Instead, the package will bolster spending on public capital (infrastructure) and help revive the economy. The infrastructure spending also will lead to expanded private investment opportunities and thus increased spending on complementary private capital. The recovery of the economy also will increase business confidence. According to this line of reasoning, the private investment demand curve will shift to the right, as from ID_1 to ID_2 in Figure 30.8 (Macro Figure 13.8). That rightward shift hopefully will swamp any crowding out caused by a rising interest rate.

8. Last Word: The Leading Indicators (page 623; Macro page 270)

The (composite) index of leading economic indicators (LEI) dropped sharply beginning in July 2007 and generally continued to fall through the months leading up to the start of the recession in December 2007. In this case, the LEI provided some forewarning of the recession. The index leveled off between March 2008 and June 2008, but then plummeted rapidly from June 2008 through November 2008. This correctly forecasted the severe decline in real GDP (–6.3 percent in annual terms) that occurred in the fourth quarter of 2008.

Chapter 31 (Macro Chapter 14): Money and Banking

1. Introduction (page 629; Macro page 276)

Our statement at the bottom of page 629 and the top of page 630 (Macro pages 276 and 277) seems particularly relevant to the current recession and is worth repeating:

> When the monetary system is working properly, it provides the lifeblood of the circular flows of income and expenditures. A well-functioning monetary system helps the economy achieve both full employment and the efficient use of

resources. A malfunctioning monetary system distorts the allocation of resources and creates severe fluctuations in the economy's levels of output, employment, and prices.

"Malfunctioning" is too gentle an adjective to describe the monetary system in late 2007 and 2008. In the Last Word on the mortgage debt crisis at the end of Chapter 33 (Macro Chapter 16), we discuss the origins of the financial crisis. It would be helpful to you to read that Last Word now (pages 682–683; Macro pages 328–329), and then return to this update.

The problems described in the Last Word relate to *securitization*, the process of slicing up and bundling groups of loans, mortgages, corporate bonds, or other financial debts into distinct new securities. These securities are then sold to financial investors, who purchase them to obtain the interest payments and the eventual return of principal generated by the underlying securities. For example, mortgage loans provided to subprime borrowers—people with below-average credit histories—were bundled together as mortgage-backed securities (MBSs) and sold to private investors and to government entities. These securities were attractive to many private investors and financial institutions because they offered higher interest rates than securities backed by less-risky mortgages.

Once created, loan-backed securities are bought and sold in financial markets just like other securities such as stocks and bonds. These sorts of securities can therefore end up worldwide in the investment portfolios of banks, thrifts, insurance companies, and pensions, as well as in personal accounts.

To reduce the risk for holders of these securities, a few large insurance companies developed other securities that the holders of loan-backed securities could purchase to insure against losses from defaults. American International Group (AIG), in particular, issued billions of dollars of collateralized default swaps (CDSs)—essentially insurance policies—that were designed to compensate the holders of loan-backed securities if the loans underlying their loan-backed securities went into default and did not pay off. Thus, these CDSs became yet another investment security exposed to mortgage-loan risk.

Securitization is so widespread and critical to the modern financial system that it is sometimes referred to as the shadow banking system. All sorts of securities backed by loans or other securities are issued, bought, sold, and resold each day in a process that helps keep credit flowing to the households and businesses that rely on it for their personal and business needs.

Sounds good, right? But what happens if the value of one of the types of loans (say, mortgages) that underlies the securitization process unexpectedly plunges? And what happens if some of the largest holders of the securities based on these mortgages happen to be major U.S. financial institutions that are vitally important to the day-to-day financing of the credit needed to keep the American economy running smoothly? And what if the main insurer of these securities (AIG) is the largest insurance company not only in the United States but in the world?

All three "what ifs?" happened! As explained in Chapter 33's Last Word, interest rates on adjustable-rate mortgages increased and house prices fell. Borrowers who had made relatively small down payments on home purchases or had cashed out home equity through refinancing discovered that they owed more on their mortgages than their properties were worth. As interest rates adjusted upward and the economy slowed, borrowers began falling behind on their monthly mortgage payments. Lenders began to foreclose on many houses while other borrowers literally handed in their house keys and walked away.

Near bankruptcy, mortgage-lender Countrywide was absorbed by Bank of America. IndyMac bank was shut down by Federal regulators, with its assets transferred to other banks. Washington Mutual bank was forced into a government-arranged takeover by JPMorgan Chase. Wachovia found refuge from bankruptcy through absorption by Wells Fargo.

Because of widespread securitization, the exposure to the growing problem of loan defaults moved well beyond the direct mortgage lenders. Securities firms and investment banks that held large amounts of loan-backed securities also began to suffer huge losses. Merrill Lynch lost more in two years than it made in the prior decade and was rescued at a fire-sale price by Bank of America. Lehman Brothers, a major holder of mortgage-backed securities, had to declare bankruptcy. Goldman Sachs, Morgan Stanley, and other financial firms rushed to become bank holding companies in order to qualify for U.S. Treasury and Federal Reserve bailout loans available only to banks and bank holding companies. Citibank needed huge infusions of Federal government funds to survive. Insurance company AIG suffered massive losses since it had not set aside sufficient reserves to pay off the unexpectedly large losses that accrued on the insurance policies that it had sold to holders of mortgage-backed securities.

In late 2008 Congress passed the Troubled Asset Relief Program (TARP), which allocated $700 billion to the Treasury Department to use in bailing out critical financial firms. As of March 2009, the Federal government and Federal Reserve had spent $170 billion just keeping AIG afloat. Other major recipients of TARP funds were Citibank, Bank of America, and JPMorgan Chase.

In March 2009, the U.S. Treasury continued its bail-out efforts by revealing the details of a public-private initiative designed to encourage qualified investors to buy risky loan-based assets from financial institutions. Once removed from the troubled financial institutions, these "toxic assets" (or "legacy assets") would then trade in separate, tightly regulated financial markets.

2. Fed Functions and the Money Supply (page 638; Macro page 285)

Observe that one of the Fed's functions is to lend money when needed to banks and thrifts. We point out that in times of financial emergencies, the Fed serves as a lender of last resort to critical parts of the U.S. financial industry. The Fed has been highly active in lending money to the financial industry during the Severe Contraction. We will list the many new and creative ways that the Fed has done this in our update on monetary policy (Chapter 33; Macro Ch 16).

3. Table 31.1: Major U.S. Financial Institutions (page 640; Macro Table 14.1, page 287)

The upheaval in the financial services industry has greatly altered Table 31.1 (Macro Table 14.1) since August 2008. This is particularly true of column 3, "Examples." Here are the changes needed to make the examples current as of March 2009:

- In the row for Commercial banks, remove Wachovia, which was acquired by Wells Fargo.
- In the Thrifts row, remove Washington Mutual, which was acquired by JPMorgan Chase; remove Golden West (owned by Wachovia) because Wachovia was acquired by Wells Fargo.
- In the row for Securities firms, note that Merrill Lynch is now part of Bank of America; remove Lehman Brothers because it went bankrupt.
- In the row for Investment banks, note that Goldman Sachs and Morgan Stanley opted to become bank holding companies (commercial banks) so they could avail themselves of loans from the Federal Reserve.

Chapter 32 (Macro Chapter 15): Money Creation

1. Last Word: The Bank Panics of 1930 to 1933 (page 656; Macro page 303)

Unlike the 1930s, the current financial crisis has not included major runs on commercial bank deposits. To help prevent runs, the FDIC in October 2008 increased its insurance coverage for commercial bank accounts from $100,000 per account to $250,000 per account. At the same time, the Fed took lender-of-last-resort actions to make sure banks had adequate reserves. In fact, bank reserves were increased so much that in February 2009 the U.S. fractional reserve system had more reserves than checkable deposits! There was no multiple destruction of the nation's money supply as had occurred in the 1930s. The problem was simply unwillingness by banks to increase lending in an economic climate in which nearly all loans were perceived as being quite risky.

Chapter 33 (Macro Chapter 16): Interest Rates and Monetary Policy

1. The Demand for Money (page 661; Macro page 308)

The transaction demand for money fell during the Severe Contraction because of the decline in nominal GDP, but the asset demand for money increased. Given the losses that investors were experiencing on assets such as real estate and stocks, many investors were content to leave money uninvested in their checking accounts, knowing it was safe and secure due to FDIC insurance.

Viewed through Figure 33.1 (page 662; Macro Figure 16.1, page 309), the transactions demand curve D_t shifted to the left and the asset demand curve D_a shifted to the right. Because the Fed so substantially increased the money supply, the resulting rightward shift of the money supply curve S_m overpowered any demand change and reduced the real interest rate.

2. The Consolidated Balance Sheet of the Federal Reserve Banks (page 663; Macro page 310)

The consolidated balance sheet of the 12 Federal Reserve banks changed markedly during the Severe Contraction. Total Fed assets rose from the $885,097 million shown in the February 14, 2008, balance sheet in Table 33.1 (page 664; Macro Table 16.1, page 311) to $1,902,798 million in March 5, 2009. This increase reflected a huge rise in the amount of securities (U.S. securities, mortgage-backed securities, and others) owned by the Federal Reserve. In undertaking its monetary policy and its lender-of-last-resort functions, the Fed bought these securities from financial institutions—purposely increasing the liquidity of the financial system. The Fed also increased its loans to financial institutions, particularly by lending through the term auction facility discussed in this chapter. Because term auction loans are "owed to" the Fed, the accounting credits for them are assets on the Fed's balance sheet.

On the liability side, the reserves of commercial banks jumped from $11,312 million to a whopping $619,713 million. To make sure they were liquid and the funds were safe, banks placed much of the proceeds from selling securities to the Fed into their respective reserve accounts at the Fed. This inflow was strengthened because the Fed began paying interest on the reserves that banks were holding at the Fed. Previously (and as stated in the book), no interest was paid on these reserves.

As we have indicated, in March 2009 total bank reserves exceeded total checkable deposits held by the banks. Because of the duress in the financial system, the fractional reserve system voluntarily and temporarily became a 100-percent-plus reserve system! As a result, banks in March 2009 had substantial excess reserves that could be used to increase lending once the banks became more certain of their own financial viability and the likelihood that newly issued loans would be paid back.

3. Targeting the Federal Funds Rate (page 670; Macro page 317)

The Fed has been able to target and achieve a low Federal funds rate. As stated in the book, between September 2007 and April 2008, the Fed lowered its target Federal funds rate from 5.25 percent to 2 percent.

In October 2008, the Fed reduced the Federal funds target rate to 1.5 percent; in October 2008, to 1 percent; and in December 2008, to the range from 0 percent to 0.25 percent. Viewed through Figure 33.3 (page 671; Macro Figure 16.3, page 318), the Fed pushed the supply of Federal funds curve downward (increased the supply of Federal funds) in order to lower the actual Federal funds rate to its target level.

The Fed succeeded in its efforts through open-market operations (buying U.S. securities from banks). That partially explains the huge increase in securities on the Fed's balance sheet (discussed in our update of Chapter 30). Of greater significance, the Fed greatly increased its auctioning of reserves through its term auction facility. As of March 4, 2009, the Fed held $495 billion of term auction credits, meaning that it had injected $495 billion of additional reserves into the system through this facility.

4. Figure 33.4: The Prime Interest Rate and the Federal Funds Rate in the United States (page 672; Macro Figure 16.4, page 319)

The decline in the Federal funds rate to near zero dropped the prime interest rate. In December 2007, the prime interest rate stood at 7.3 percent. By February 2009, it had declined to 3.25 percent.

5. Recent U.S. Monetary Policy (page 678; Macro page 325)

Along with reducing the Federal funds rate and thereby lowering the prime interest rate (as just discussed), the Fed has created extraordinary and highly creative lender-of-last-resort facilities to maintain liquidity in the financial system. These facilities involve new procedures and capabilities in addition to open-market operations, the discount rate, the reserve requirement, and the term auction facility. All are designed to keep credit flowing in the economy.

- **Primary Dealer Credit Facility (PDCF).** Provides overnight loans to primary dealers who are willing to post loan-backed securities as collateral. (The Fed keeps the collateral on any loan that is not repaid on time.) Primary dealers are the 16 major financial institutions that the Fed uses to buy and sell U.S. securities.
- **Term Securities Lending Facility (TSLF).** Lends U.S. securities to primary dealers for one-month terms to promote liquidity in the markets for these securities. The financial institutions obtain the securities through participating in competitive single-bid auctions.
- **Asset-Backed Commercial Paper Money Market Mutual Fund Liquidity Facility.** Provides loans to U.S. banks and thrifts to finance their purchases of *commercial paper* from money market mutual funds. Commercial paper is vital for financing the day-to-day operations of businesses and consists of asset-backed, short-term IOUs that are mainly issued by corporations.
- **Commercial Paper Funding Facility (CPFF).** Purchases commercial paper to support the commercial paper market and therefore the short-term credit needs of businesses.
- **Money Market Investor Funding Facility (MMIFF).** Provides funding support to a private-sector initiative designed to ensure the liquidity of U.S. money market mutual funds. Many Americans rely on money market funds as low-risk investments.
- **Term Asset-Backed Securities Loan Facility (TALF).** Helps households and businesses with their credit needs by providing funding support for asset-backed securities collateralized by student loans, auto loans, credit card loans, and loans guaranteed by the Small Business Administration (SBA).
- **Interest Payments on Reserves.** Bolsters the profitability of banks by paying interest on the reserves they hold in their vaults or in the Federal Reserve Banks.

6. Cyclical Asymmetry (page 679; Macro page 329)

Monetary policy has run squarely into the problem of cyclical asymmetry that is discussed in the book. The Fed has created billions of dollars of excess reserves that have driven down the Federal funds rate to 0.2 percent (March 2009). The prime interest rate has fallen from 7.3 percent (December 2007) to 3.25 percent (March 2009). Nevertheless, lending by banks was sluggish throughout the first 15 months of the recession. As noted, the banks are fearful that the loans they make will not be paid back. Consequently, they have been content to hold reserves at the Federal Reserve banks.

This is the "pushing on a string" problem that the Bank of Japan (BOJ) encountered in the 1990s (Consider This, page 679; Macro page 330). Like the BOJ, the Fed has lowered the nominal interest rate to near zero and the economy is still reeling. The Fed has encountered a *liquidity trap* in which adding more liquidity to banks has little or no positive effect on lending, borrowing, investment, or aggregate demand.

This liquidity trap was a primary reason why public policy attempts to expand demand turned so significantly and forcefully toward fiscal policy in 2009. Recall our discussion of the American Recovery and Reinvestment Act of 2009, which authorized the infusion of $787 billion of new tax cuts and government spending in 2009 and 2010.

Chapter 34 (Macro Chapter 17): Financial Economics

1. Risk (page 694; Macro page 341)

The large losses suffered by investors in the financial markets in 2007 and 2008 demonstrate that all investment decisions are affected by the presence of nondiversifiable risk (or systemic risk). The difficulties in the real estate and other financial markets and the sharp economic downturn reduced actual returns on nearly every class of investment. Only a few assets such as U.S. Treasury securities, other government-backed securities, and gold were spared.

2. Figure 34.1: The Security Market Line (page 698; Macro Figure 17.1, page 345)

The special circumstances of the financial markets during the Severe Contraction provide an excellent illustration of both the impact of Federal Reserve actions and the idea of *time-varying risk premium*. The latter is the reality that the premium demanded by investors to take on risk may vary from one period (and one set of economic circumstances) to another period (and a different set of economic circumstances).

The Federal Reserve used expansionary monetary policy during this period to lower interest rates, including the interest rates of short-term U.S. government bonds. Because the risk-free interest rate earned by these securities locates the vertical intercept of the Security Market Line (SML), the actual SML for the economy shifted downward from that shown in Figure 34.1 (Macro Figure 17.1). This decline would be portrayed as the opposite of the upward shift that we illustrate in Figure 34.4 (page 700; Macro Figure 17.4, page 347).

But wouldn't we expect stock market prices to rise when the risk-free rate of return falls? That certainly did *not* happen in 2007 and 2008. Yes, normally, stock market prices rise when the risk-free interest rate falls. But during this unusual period, investors became very fearful about losses from investments in general and began to look for any place of safety. As their appetite for risk decreased, they demanded a much higher rate of compensation for taking on any particular level of risk. In terms of Figure 34.4 (Macro Figure 17.4), the slope of the SML greatly increased. Thus, between the Fed's deliberate reduction of the risk-free rate and investors' diminished appetite for risk, two things happened at once to the SML: (1) its intercept (the risk-free rate) dramatically fell and (2) the SML became much steeper. In Figure 34.1 (Macro Figure 17.1), this would be shown by a much steeper SML emanating from a much lower point on the vertical axis.

The increase in the slope of the SML, however, overwhelmed the decline in the intercept. Investors sold off stocks, which greatly reduced stock prices, even though the risk-free interest rate fell.

Chapter 35 (Macro Chapter 18): Extending the Analysis of Aggregate Supply

1. Recession and the Extended AD-AS Model (page 712; Macro page 359)

A long-lasting and deep recession such as the Severe Contraction places downward pressure on wages and other input prices. Eventually these declines will shift the short-run aggregate supply curve to the right, as from AS_1 to AS_2 in Figure 35.5 (page 712; Macro Figure 18.5, page 359). In theory, the price level therefore will fall (deflation will occur) as the economy moves along AD_2 from a recessionary point like *b* to a point like *c*. At the lower price level, more real output will be demanded, which means that real GDP will "self-correct" back to potential output and full employment. But, as stated in the book, most economists believe this process will be excruciatingly slow and extremely costly in terms of lost output. Also, uncertain "wait-it-out" solutions to serious economic problems are often not politically viable. Most economists therefore support active monetary and fiscal policy to try to restore full-employment output via rightward shifts of the aggregate demand curve.

2. The Phillips Curve (page 714; Macro page 361)

The current recession is following the general pattern of the Phillips Curve (Figure 35.8a on page 715; Macro Figure 18.8, page 362). The unemployment rate increased to 8.5 percent in February 2009 while the rate of inflation for 2008 declined to a very low 0.1 percent on a December-to-December basis.

3. Taxation and Aggregate Supply (page 720; Macro page 367)

The tax rebates of 2008 and the tax cuts for low-income and moderate-income Americans contained in the 2009 stimulus package were structured more towards increasing aggregate demand (and redistributing income) than expanding aggregate supply. They were mainly demand-side tax cuts, not the supply-side tax cuts discussed in this section.

Chapter 36 (Macro Chapter 19): Current Issues in Macro Theory and Policy

1. What Causes Macro Instability? (page 727; Macro page 374)

The current recession seems to fit the mainstream view (page 727; Macro page 374) as opposed to the real-business cycle view (page 729; Macro page 376). Economists with monetarist leanings, however, cite monetary factors as the main cause of the financial crisis, which in turn led to the Severe Contraction. They argue that the Federal Reserve flooded the economy with too much money and held interest rates too low for too long in promoting recovery from the 2001 recession. As evidence, they point out that the Fed's monetary policy during this period diverged greatly from the Taylor rule (Last Word, page 738; Macro page 385), which, if it had been adhered to by the Fed, would have led to higher Federal funds rates and prime interest rates. In this line of reasoning, the excess money and low interest rates contributed to the bubble in the housing market. When that bubble burst, the resulting loan defaults set in motion the forces that produced the recession.

All economists agree that the bursting of the housing bubble created a set of forces that led to the recession. Most economists acknowledge that a too-loose monetary policy may have contributed to the bubble but also cite the large international capital inflows received by the United States during this period. These inflows drove down interest rates and helped to fuel the housing bubble. Other factors such as "pass-the-risk" lending practices and poorly designed and enforced financial regulations came into play. Economic historians will need to sort out the causal factors. Usually they find that a combination of factors, none critical by itself, come together to cause major unexpected economic events like the Severe Contraction.

Chapter 37 (Macro Chapter 20; Micro Chapter 23): International Trade

1. Some Key Facts (page 744; Macro page 391; Micro page 467)

A key fact of the Severe Contraction is that it has diminished world trade. Exports have collapsed in some countries, along with lower imports. In fact, world trade has dropped by the greatest extent since the Second World War. For example, 2008 saw exports fall 35 percent in Japan and 21 percent in Germany. These sharp declines in international trade imply fewer world gains from specialization based on comparative advantage.

2. Increased Domestic Employment Argument (page 758; Macro page 405; Micro page 481)

Arguments for trade protections often are louder than usual during a severe recession. Widespread unemployment understandably leads interest groups and some elected officials to argue that tariffs and other trade restrictions are necessary to reduce imports and thereby stem domestic job losses.

These policies are sometimes called *beggar-thy-neighbor policies* because they try to improve one's own economy at the expense of foreign economies. But, as pointed out in the book, this "logic" fails because it is an example of the *fallacy of composition*: What is true for one nation acting alone is not true for all nations acting simultaneously. In particular, if other nations are free to retaliate, then your trade restrictions will quickly generate successive rounds of retaliation by other nations. Their restrictions collapse your exports, quickly offsetting any benefits you hoped to achieve by reducing your imports. World trade plummets and only then does everyone understand that imposing trade restrictions was a huge mistake.

In constructing the $787 billion stimulus package in 2009, Congress inserted a provision that all projects use materials supplied by U.S. producers. The idea was to increase domestic employment. But when other nations threatened retaliation against American exports, the language in the law was reworked to say, ". . . consistent U.S. obligations under international agreements." Those treaties limit "buy American" clauses such as these and cushion the impact of the prohibition.

Put bluntly, the United States cannot cure its current maladies by enacting tariffs and passing "buy American" laws. Other countries will simply retaliate. Because the United States is among the world's largest exporters, U.S. exports will plummet and employment in industries in which the United States has a comparative advantage will sink. (The colorful quotation by Paul Krugman in the Consider This box on page 756 [Macro page 403; Micro page 479] is particularly relevant! Give it another look.)

3. The World Trade Organization (page 759; Macro page 406; Micro page 482)

The Doha Round of international trade negotiations is still stalled. For reasons just cited, periods of recession are not at all conducive for achieving agreements to reduce tariffs and liberalize trade.

Chapter 38 (Macro Chapter 21): The Balance of Payments, Exchange Rates, and Trade Deficits

1. Flexible Exchange Rates (page 769; Macro page 416)

The international value of the U.S. dollar has fluctuated but generally increased during the recession. At the start of the recession in December 2007, a U.S. dollar could buy 0.69 euro, 0.5 pound, and 1 Canadian dollar. By March 2009, a U.S. dollar could buy 0.79 euro, 0.71 British pound, and 1.29 Canadian dollars.

The appreciation of the dollar resulted from two key factors. First, the United States entered its recession considerably sooner than our trading partners. As U.S. income declined, so did U.S. imports. The decline in imports meant less demand for the foreign currencies needed to obtain imports. The decline in the demand for these foreign currencies resulted in their depreciation relative to the dollar.

Second, as financial systems around the world began to destabilize, foreign investors increasingly became fearful about holding investments that had previously been considered safe, such as corporate bonds issued by companies in their own nations. The "flight to safety" by foreign investors led them to buy secure U.S. government securities. To obtain these bonds, they needed to purchase U.S. dollars. The resulting increased demand for dollars boosted the international value of the dollar. That is, the dollar appreciated.

These two factors overpowered other factors such as low U.S. interest rates and low expected returns on U.S. stocks, bonds, and real estate. By themselves, these other factors would have depreciated the dollar.

2. Recent U.S. Trade Deficits (page 778; Macro page 425)

U.S. imports usually fall by more than U.S. exports in recessions and therefore recessions tend to reduce U.S. goods deficits, goods and services deficits, and current account deficits. Preliminary data for 2008 confirms this general pattern. Although the goods deficit in 2008 was roughly the same as it was in 2007, the goods and services deficit (Figure 38.4a) fell from $700 billion in 2007 to $681 billion. The current account deficit (Figure 38.4b) dropped from $731 billion in 2007 to $673 billion in 2008. These data are preliminary, however, and you can update them through the U.S. Department of Commerce Web site, **www.bea.gov**. Simply select Balance of Payments.